# THE CONCEALMENT OF ENDLESS LIGHT

# PRAISE

"Elegantly crafted, beautifully philosophical, and passionately devoted to exploring the profundity of earthly life, *The Concealment of Endless Light* chronicles a quest for the divine amid the ordinary. Never holier-than-thou, the speaker in November's poems is always conscious of the ways he's failed his family, himself, and his God. Nonetheless, he persists in reaching out to the divine to illuminate the experiences of a soul in a body."
**—Maria Mazziotti Gillan**

"How does Yehoshua November do it? How does he balance the lofty and mundane with such grace? This remarkable poet finds mystery in kitchens and hardware stores, dry cleaners and classrooms. In the same breath, he describes a soul's journey and eating breakfast with his children. In this world of ours where human beings do horrible things to each other, November looks for souls inside bodies. Certainly, that gives him a perspective on our species. But there is something else, too. Mystics have been trying to 'nail' this something for generations, to name it. November answers this metaphysical challenge—he names the unnamable—via his skillful use of figurative language. But there is more, yet. Friends, these days in our country, we go to school to learn to make sentences and to divide and multiply numbers. But where can we learn awe and wonderment? The answer is November's humane and deeply searching poems. He has a wisdom which is necessary if one is to travel from one day to the next. November is one of our most brilliant Jewish American poets of this moment."
**—Ilya Kaminsky**

"A wonderful poet with a unique vision and distinct voice, Yehoshua November opens worlds within worlds. In *The Concealment of Endless Light*, he describes poetry as 'that profession of rowing / through the rivers of the heart / with oars made of memory / and sadness,' though in his case memory and speculation are illuminated by the daily wakings of a father and husband scratching out a living as a teacher and backlit by the soul, despite 'a Divine concealment whose diameter is greater / than infinity.' In a moving poem about the Pittsburgh synagogue shooting, November gathers the dead around him on a street where the 'Jews of Pittsburgh / stand in the rain / holding candles' while 'eleven souls ascend to the region of mystery / then swoop down to hover, incandescently, over their former lives,' consecrating a place where 'no one can explain how [the body] limps forward / but has not faltered.' Neither does this poet falter, but moves forward with dignity and grace."
**—Dorianne Laux**

# THE CONCEALMENT OF ENDLESS LIGHT

Yehoshua November

ORISON
BOOKS

*The Concealment of Endless Light*


ISBN: 978-1-949039-50-4

Orison Books
PO Box 8385
Asheville, NC 28814
www.orisonbooks.com

Cover Art: "Aleph, Before Creation" by Dov Laimon. Used by permission of the artist.
Cover design by Luke Hankins and Addison Skigen.

Manufactured in the U.S.A.

ORISON
BOOKS

# Contents

## IV



## V

# Notes on the Soul

1.

Like one descending
the stairs to the supply room
for a paperclip
but pausing
beneath the door frame,
a soul enters
a particular body
and cannot
remember why.

2.

*If there is no such thing as a soul—*
my blue-haired student,
who said she'd never have a child,
wrote in her notebook—
*then how does my mother know,*
*from hundreds of miles away,*
*when I am sad?*

3.

Part of the soul
resides inside
the body,
which resides inside
the world—
the way the memory
of a kiss
circles in the mind
of a prisoner
walking laps
around the prison courtyard.

# I

## Teachers and Students

1.

It was when she pulled out her chair
after entering midway
through our fourth class—
muttering what at first sounded like a lie
about struggling to find parking—
that I realized my Vietnamese student
had only one hand.

She wrote a short piece
on her high school music teacher's prediction
her prosthetic
could not summon the pressure she'd need
to squeeze out the staccato notes
at the upcoming violin recital.

2.

Strangely, often,
teachers' most hurtful comments
are also untrue.

3.

At the dining room table, I lost my temper
after one of my sons misread
a word in a Hebrew prayer
we'd practiced a hundred times.
*I'm a stupid person.*
*What do you want from me?*

4.

*When you pray, do not*
*make your prayers routine*
*but an entreaty of mercy and a supplication*
*before the Almighty,*
Rabbi Shimon would say.

5.

All semester, the sorority sister
tossed her dark hair,
checked her phone, whispered to her friends
in light tones.
In her final portfolio, a poem about her attempt,
in ninth grade, to OD on Aspirin
after learning the upperclassman
she'd given herself to
had been playing
*First Senior to Sleep with a Freshman.*

6.

In one of my earliest memories,
I am a boy whose father
has brought him to the town rabbi
for thinking lowly of himself
after earning a B- on an exam
on the book of Genesis.
In his basement office, the large rabbi leans toward me:
*Don't compare yourself to your classmates.*

7.

A professor takes a sip of coffee
from his earthenware mug,
writes “Fascinating” in the margins
of a student paper
without reading a word.

8.

In his notebook, on the page
where he wrote about finding
his father’s “ugly blue body,”
my student’s script turns very large
but barely legible.

9.

It’s said that at age six—
a slow learner with prodigious stepbrothers
and a famous rabbinic father—
Maimonides ran away from home,
opened the ark of the local synagogue,
pleaded, saw sparks,
and awoke with a photographic memory.

10.

On my commute to teach courses
in Brooklyn and New Brunswick,
I listen to the recorded lectures of a rabbi
who recently passed away.
Between teaching the technical verses
on the Tabernacle’s construction,
he offers impersonations of the yeshiva cook,

Montreal, circa 1960,
and tells stories of his father's rabbinate in Newark.
In one, a drunken former S.S. officer
follows the spiritual leader down Union Street,
begging for Divine exoneration.
"I will not forgive you,"
the rabbi answers, each time.

11.

Once, I returned a failing paper
to a front tackle,
who stood up to his full 6'7" height,
rustled the pages, and bolted out of the room
in his scarlet sweatsuit.
A moment later he returned
to grab his backpack, flip the light switch,
and disappear again.

Winter's muted daylight
entered through the windows
along the back wall of the remedial classroom.

In the semi-darkness,
seventeen faces gazed up at me.

# The Buttonhook

My son sprinted to each traffic light
in his black hat and dark Sabbath suit
while the elderly congregation two miles away
waited for him to lead morning prayers.

Moments earlier, after my final attempt to wake him,
I stood at the bottom of the steps,
unleashing dire predictions about how he'd fare
in yeshiva high school the following year—

until his mother whispered in his ear,
and suddenly he was in the foyer,
putting on a scarf and a coat,
then running full stride past the mini-mart
and corner gas station and doubling back
until I'd caught up to him,

reminding me of a loyal pet
or the buttonhook play my father called
in our backyard football huddle:
*Run straight out, then turn back.*
*The ball will be waiting for you.*

A week earlier I'd screamed
through the bathroom door,
a rehash of the year's arguments
softened by a thousand wooden fibers between us,
the way, the mystics say,
Divine severity filters through
countless intervening worlds
before it reaches us
in diminished measure.

Oh, the terrible words I said
about things he couldn't help.

And now he is crossing the bridge
over the Hackensack River's dingy waters,
Saturday morning traffic swooshing by, wind
stinging my eyes, and I race ahead
to catch up with him.

# Hearing Roy Orbison in a Mikvah in Salem, MA

*In dreams I walk with you,*
Roy Orbison crooned
from the speakers above the indoor pool,
at the Holiday Inn,
steam rising as I resurfaced
from beneath the chlorine waters
of the makeshift mikvah.

If slightly rearranged, the letters
in the word *tevilah*, ritual immersion
in a body of water,
spell *habitul*, the self's dissolution
in the face of the Divine.

"He was quiet, self-effacing,"
Orbison's biographers noted.
Bathed in spotlight,
he hid behind Wayfarer sunglasses
and never danced on stage.

To submerge beneath the water,
the mystics add,
is to return to the Divine womb,
the way the soul returns to the Heavens each night
as the body dozes.

Claudette—
Orbison's first wife, whom he divorced
after her infidelities with the contractor who'd built
the couple's Hendersonville home,
and whom he remarried a year later—

died in the singer's arms shortly after
her motorcycle collided
with a truck pulling onto South Water Avenue.

It was 6AM. I had the mivkah to myself.
I heard desperation in the operatic voice that hailed
from Vernon, Texas.
I was in Salem for a panel
on 21st-century devotional poetry.

Like the soul climbing
while the body reposes,
Orbison's voice rose higher
than the sopranos.
*In dreams I talk with you.*
"The lyrics came to me
as I slept," Orbison claimed.
"Words I wrote down upon waking."

Our panel asked what it meant
for a contemporary poet
to speak to our Father in Heaven in this millennium.
Mostly, we do not know.

Two of Orbison's sons, 6 and 11, died
when the Hendersonville home
went up in flames. Orbison's second wife,
Barbara, passed away
on the 23rd anniversary of the singer's death.

Once, three thousand years ago,
Moses asked God,
Who could have made the world any way He wanted,
why He'd created suffering.

Moses, whose name means
“one drawn from the water,”
was the only prophet
to speak with God face to face,
that is, in a waking state.
But he heard only staticky silence—
oceanic, wavelike,
the crackling of a turntable
following a song’s final note.

## On the World's Continuity Via Divine Speech

God is like a celebrity
making small talk
at a dinner party.
Everyone hangs on His words,
and if He were to stop speaking,
the evening would end.

# Impossibly

The way, the mystics say,
the higher parts of the soul
transcend the body,
hover above,
you sit at the dinner table
in turquoise skirt and dark blouse
surrounded by five children.
Potato flakes on the floor, fish sticks
and ketchup smears on the tablecloth,
you read a book about sharing.
Your voice—calm, measured—floats above
the disorder after a morning three daughters
hollered in the upstairs hallway,
an afternoon two sons pierced
a park's peace
until a Chinese stranger slid
the younger one's bike chain
back on track. Your voice
rises above the dining room,
flows from your dark body
into the air
for five young faces
rapt, impossibly, in attention
and wonderment.

# This Summer Day

Our Father in Heaven is kind,
but will He be kind the way we want Him to be?

One day, the children will be grown.
Hopefully, some pride

to go along with the regrets.
Some sun, as on this summer day:

The kids swim outside in the plastic pool.
Our oldest daughter overseas with your parents.

You, in a white top and tan skirt,
run your hand over the surface of the water.

How you have remained beautiful
over these fourteen years,

beautiful and optimistic, despite
the nights in the small apartment

with great fears, carrying cups of water
to four sleepless children

as I commuted across the bridge to teach another section
of English Composition at the night college.

How the world gets larger

and smaller—like the moon,
each month—

larger and smaller.

# II

# Notes on the Tzimtzum

1.

Once, on a bus from Jerusalem to Ein Gedi,
I saw a man place his hand
over his bare head
and recite the blessing
over water.

2.

One can't use his hand
as a head covering,
the Rabbis conclude,
because one can't cover
oneself with oneself.

3.

Since the Divine hand hides
that everything stems out of the Divine,
when God looks at the world—
like moss growing over moss—
He sees only Divinity.

4.

The Jew without a yarmulke
placed the cap
on his water bottle
and resumed watching a YouTube
on black holes.

5.

In this world, Hashem conceals
His omnipresence, His infinite light—
His power to hide eclipsing His power to reveal.

6.

In this world,
we ride buses through a Divine concealment
whose diameter is greater
than infinity,
we sip water
beside a dam
that holds back
endless light.

## *I FELT LIKE I HAD WALKED THROUGH THE STREETS OF JERUSALEM IN AN EARLIER LIFE*

In a desk, I find a printout of an email from my grandfather,
written in all caps at the end of the last millennium,
a response to a message I'd sent him when I was 18,
studying in a yeshiva in Israel, burdened by doubts.
Coming from a secular man, a former army aviation mechanic
and auto parts warehouse owner,
his answer surprises me.
His P.S., a dated fear or another affirmation of faith.
*DID YOU SEE THE WEATHER CHANNEL'S FATALISTIC*
*REPORTS ABOUT EL NIÑO?*
*WHAT DO WE UNDERSTAND ABOUT THE WIND?*

# In the Dream, My Father Reprimanded Me for Wearing Earmuffs Indoors

Had I reminded him
of the crumbling house,
Lenox Road, Brooklyn—
his three sisters sleeping in their coats
December–February?
His father drifting from work
at one factory to another,
a stint as "head engineer"
at the Now and Later Toffee Warehouse?
Had my subconscious created the perfect scenario
to irk him? Erased the late-night hours
he'd spent under the library fluorescents?

In the dream, my father parked the blue station wagon
in the garage behind the house
and walked up the icy path,
having performed a tricky, all-night
breech delivery.
I sat at the kitchen table,
enveloped in my baseball-card-fruity-pebbles-childhood,
oblivious to a father coming in from the cold,
shouting to his son
to remove his earmuffs
and face life's cantankerous music.
Seeing I did not hear,
he removed his dark overcoat and ascended
the staircase in a single great stride,
his body swallowed in sunlight
as his foot touched the landing.

# Zaida Sydney

*for my grandfather*

*Ow, you beaned me*, he howled,
hopping on one foot in our backyard to shake off
the pain of my pitch. How stately his tall frame
as he assumed a batter's stance at 75
in his signature brown pants and yellow shirt.
He laughed high pitched at jokes on TV
and the autographs he forged on our baseball cards.

When we'd stay in his small Brooklyn apartment,
half the square footage taken
by his dark room,
I'd sleep between him and my grandmother,
a short woman who battled
her own Russian sadness
but supported him ceaselessly.
His long arm draped over my frame,
I'd turn to spy,
under folding-chair night stand,
bottles of vodka, comic books,
a journal filled with her poems.

When the principal of our yeshiva in Rochester
left town for his son's wedding,
my friends and I
escaped to New York and landed
in Zaida's apartment.
We returned from a movie,
pizza, ice cream floats,
to listen to my father reprimand us

on the answering machine,
Zaida's laugh equally uproarious
with each replaying.

He brought us to his dark room,
projected a midnight slide show
of bright yellow bees nesting on green stems,
Monarch butterflies opening
white-tipped wings against purple hydrangeas.
Each image touched up
until the world appeared
the way he saw it.

## Re-creation Ex Nihilo Via Divine Utterance

It's the Principle of the Cosmic Hardware Store:
The floor will hold not because of sound construction

but because, each moment, the floorboards are re-spoken
into existence. Indeed, the Law of Conservation of Matter

would disappear from every textbook
were it not announced again and again

over Heaven's staticky intercom.
One must train oneself, therefore,

to call the world's bluff, train oneself,
upon boarding a plane, for example,

to believe it is safe not because of the pilot's
credentials, the ground crew's inspection, the expert

wiring of the control panel. The titanium alloy,
the screws fastening the fuselage,

the snow, the fog, the otherness
of the passenger in the window seat,

their nose ring and neo-gothic novel—
all continuously articulated

out of nothingness
and into being

like the cup of seltzer with a wedge of lime
the flight attendant's hand
extends toward you
through the cabin air—

the mystery
of creation.

# Rabbi W.

The month before my bar mitzvah,
he took the class to a Twins game at the Metrodome.
I ascended the steps behind the left-field wall
to order my first non-kosher hotdog.
When I turned from the condiment station,
contraband sausage in my mouth,
he was exiting the bathroom,
then standing in front of me:
dark suit, white shirt, loosened tie, pained eyes.
He simply returned to his seat.

The day after I'd interviewed
at a secular prep school and left
my tefillin in his classroom closet,
he said softly, *They cry each day*
*you do not wear them.*

Once, somehow, the false rumor
got out I had spread a lie
about the mother of a girl in our class
having an affair.
The junior high divided,
friends and enemies.
He gave me four quarters
and a pass to buy two sodas
from the machine in the teachers' lounge
(that foreign country),
to take her on a walk
and explain my side.

On a road trip to a yeshiva in Wisconsin,
he asked me to repeat, over and again,
my impersonation of our town's rabbi:
*Yehoshua Yaakov, can you*
*get me a cola beverage?*
Embarrassed to be standing
in his pajamas,
he told our classmates assigned to share his room,
*I'm not the same person*
*who teaches you Talmud.*

One rainy night,
the summer after eighth grade,
I answered the front door, and there he was,
needing to talk with my father
about one of his children's medical concerns.

The next month,
we moved halfway across the country.
A friend told me
he saw Rabbi W.
at the dollar store,
buying prizes for his third-grade class,
which he'd picked up in addition
to teaching the older grades,
tutoring, bar mitzvah lessons, and running a camp.

Decades later, not knowing of him, my wife
heard his daughter speak in Brooklyn
at a gathering for Jewish mothers
with hearing-impaired children.
She was deaf, learned, articulate,
a young woman of unusual humility
and grace.

# Ein Sof Radio

*after a photograph of a rabbi in a prayer shawl listening*
*to the radio, Jerusalem, 1934, photographer unknown*

And Amichai writes that the black stripes
on the prayer shawl
*come from infinity and to infinity they go.*
But the small hands
of the antique radio dial
are locked in finitude
and in finitude they will remain.

*

The mystics speak
of two Divine lenses,
higher and lower, infinite and finite,
Das Elyon and Das Tachton.

From the higher perspective,
the world relative to the Divine—
a body swallowed
in an oversized prayer shawl,
a sunray within the globe of the sun.

In the lower perspective,
each speck of dust holds
a Divine spark and God,
like a tall woman
bending to study a silver minnow,
oversees our smallest moments.

*

*My father...packed his books...*
*and all of our belongings, then sat down*
*to await instruction from his god, yes, but also*
*from a radio*, writes Li-Young Lee.
Did he mean God spoke
through the broadcaster
or that the radio and the Divine
are not one?

*

The Ark in the Holy of Holies
measured two and a half cubits long,
one and a half cubits wide...
but occupied no space in the room.
The infinite shining
through the finite. The rabbi wears a tallis
but listens to the radio.
The world does not exist.
It is an afternoon in 1934.

*

To explain the paradoxes, the Chassidic masters
speak of Atzmus,
or Essence,
a third perspective,
the lens that fuses opposites—
like a midpoint between two walls.
The higher and lower perspectives combined.

*

Once, on Simchas Torah, an elderly man
leaned toward me, scotch on his breath,

and confessed,
*I did the camera work*
*for unsavory films*
*to pay my children's Hebrew School tuition.*

Seeing a Jew in a prayer shawl and tefillin
greasing the axle of his wagon,
Reb Levi Yitzchok of Berditchev said,
*Master of the Universe,*
*even when Your people grease their axles,*
*they pray.*

*

The rabbi rests his head on his hand
to listen to the news in an 8x10 sitting room
that exists only in God's imagination.
The prayer shawl and the radio dials—
the finite parts
that pick up infinity's signal.
The channel, Ein Sof radio.

*

God hides the fact
that He is the only thing that exists
so that a man—sometimes, even a rabbi—
listens to the news,
to human voices, and believes
the world runs itself.

III

# Forty Years

Forty years on the Jewish and secular calendar.
Forty years largely devoted to the body
but, sometimes, when clarity pierces the shell—
the soul, too,
which is too strict, too narrow-minded,
according to Chassidic thought.
It always wants to attend another lecture
on the Higher and Lower Garden,
the Seven Firmaments,
ignoring the world,
the body waiting
to be sanctified.
Forty years bisected evenly:
Twenty with you, twenty before you.
And five souls pulled down into bodies.

## Prayer

Over the years,
a man forgets
his wife's
beauty,
finds himself
spellbound
by the face of another,
less beautiful,
woman. This is like one
to whom prayer
has become merely a habit.

# And I Knew Everything Would Remain Ordinary

Each morning, before sunrise,
I reviewed the mystical discourse
on Divine Providence:
*. . . the slightest movement*
*of each blade of grass*
*fulfills the Divine intent*
*of creation as a whole.*
After teaching the last course
of the day, I watched geese
ascend from the river
behind the crumbling tennis court, chanting
*life is meaningless.*

And one day, in the middle of my years,
I sat in a boardroom's plush chair,
the green eyes of the man opposite me
sparkling as he outlined an offer
not generous enough to change
my life. And on my walk
to the edge of the parking lot,
I heard a car door slam in the distance
and recalled your face—
which I had dreamt of
the whole first year of college,
when you did not hold my hand
on the grassy hill behind the dorms
but then, inexplicably, the next fall,
began to trace your toe
around my shoelace.

# The Deed

1.

Sunlight pours through the library window.
An hour's snowy drive from my family,
I grade expository essays on the overlap
between Buddhism and psychology
to pay for my children's cheder tuition,
so they can learn texts in the holy tongue
which offer a different approach
to happiness.

Raised in a home
where the Marx Brothers played anarchistic pranks
as background to family dinners,
Sam Cooke's falsetto floating up
from my father's Danish speakers,
I tried to become a Chassid.
Which texts and whose voices
do I carry
as I shuttle between yeshiva
and classes at the university?

Between driving, grading papers, the children
waking us each night,
so little time for thinking, for learning, for love.

2.

*Action*, the Rebbe taught, *is the most essential thing. The deed*
*prescribed by the Infinite One*
*the only highway*
*beyond the finite.*

*The heart of a man meditating in front of a lake*
*soars only as high*
*as the human heart can climb.*

*Yet, because it is*
*a Divine command,*
*when he hears the shofar*
*after the others have roused him, a worshiper*
*who'd fallen asleep in the middle of services*
*climbs the ladder,*
*embraces the One Without End.*

3.

Perhaps this is why
there are so few pious Jews in poetry—

that profession of rowing
through the rivers of the heart
with oars made of memory

and sadness.

4.

The walls of the Rebbe's office
absorbed sadder stories
than any other room in the world.
His heart was so full of affection,
he cried in a synagogue
full of bearded men in Brooklyn
whenever he spoke of God's hiddenness.

On my drive home tonight,
snow circles under street lights

as the sedan ahead of me inches forward.
My wife calls to say two of the children
have done something she cannot repeat
over the phone.

When she hangs up, a staticky recording of a discourse
the Rebbe delivered decades ago resumes:
*The worshiper must serve the Divine*
*even if he feels or understands nothing.*

# What About the Here and Now?

"When you die, you will meet God,"
reads the billboard
foregrounding the stretch of industrial factories
off the state highway
on my commute home each night.

*

When I was twenty-four,
I felt a great weight lift
as I walked past New Life Dry Cleaners,
Squirrel Hill snowmelt underfoot,
and first believed
in the Baal Shem Tov's conception
of Divine Providence:
Each leaf's falling,
each turn on the way down,
is prefigured in—at each moment,
governed by—
the Divine imagination.

*

The next week, a faceless force pulled me
out of my chair in the star poet's course
on Apollinaire and the French Surrealists
and placed me in a New Jersey yeshiva.
In the study hall, a rabbi, thin as a reed,
translated a Chassidic discourse
on the world's nonexistence:
*Creation relative to the Ein Sof*

*is like a sunray inside the globe of the sun itself.*
*Because everything transpires within the Divine,*
*nothing occurs*
*that is not fated.*
I sat motionless in my seat
for thirteen months.

*

Once, after the day's last prayers,
I was summoned to the payphone
in the rundown yeshiva coat closet—
rabbinical students' dusty fedoras hanging on hooks—
to hear my dark-haired wife whisper
she was pregnant
with our second child,
our first son.

*

A week before his birth,
in need of employment,
I crossed the bridge that led to Brooklyn,
mythic city of my father's childhood,
to discuss *The Metamorphosis* with twenty-year-old
seminary students just returned
from the Holy Land,
who, I suspected, would take issue with
their Czechoslovakian brother's modernist conviction
a million random factors
had come together just so
to bury his life.

*

Kafka passed away
on the First of Sivan,
anniversary of the Jewish nation's arrival
at Mount Sinai—
the day, the midrash states,
all theological debates were set aside,
and two million Jews camped in the desert
*like one man, with one heart.*

*

*The roles and faces here are unrehearsed,*
Szymborska wrote.
Still, in my nineteenth year, I spotted my intended
carrying a tray of steaming green beans
to the serving station on our first kosher kitchen shift
at the Upstate public university.
Thin arched eyebrows,
long dark hair,
a space between her front teeth,
eyes backlit by a calm radiance
I could not name.

*

Kafka's paternal grandfather, Yaakov,
was a shochet, a ritual butcher—
one who must possess exemplary fear of Heaven—
in the Czech village of Osek.
He believed in Divine Providence—
the force that stripped me from my table
in the yeshiva study hall
to explain to strangers of the opposite sex
at the Jewish night college

why an insect, once a man,
might climb a wall and cling to a photograph
of a woman in a fur coat,
cut from a glossy magazine.

*

We walk down a lane
between a corn-feed factory and a grassy field
in Postville, Iowa.
It is father-son weekend at yeshiva,
my eldest son's third high school
in three years.
At this one, the rabbis tell me
he is a good bachur, a serious student.
When I share this with him,
he looks down at the concrete path in disbelief.
When he was a boy,
I lost my temper whenever he stared off
during morning prayers, pushing away
a God I told him was close.

*

Before he was revealed
as the century's great mystic,
founder of the Chassidic movement,
the Baal Shem Tov,
known for his infinite patience,
served as a teacher's assistant in a Polish village,
walking the youngest children
to school and back.

*

Once, when I sat beside him
during evening prayers, my father,
away most nights at the hospital,
lovingly circled his thumb
around the back of my neck.

*

Kafka's mother gave birth to six children,
Franz the eldest.
Two brothers, Georg and Heinrich,
died before he was seven.
His three sisters, Gabriele, Valerie, and Ottla,
were murdered in the Holocaust.
Those who believe a Divine force
oversees every detail
are asked to explain the world's sadness,
but they can't.

# Faith

To climb each rung
of the mind,

teeter
at the top,

and then surrender
like a librarian who reaches for a book

on the highest shelf
and then breathes in

the strange and foreign air
above the ladder.

# Universal Symbol

I walk past the bullwhip and riding helmet
encased in glass at the Holocaust exhibit
in the basement of the college library.
Two floors above,
students watch Netflix on laptops
and cell phones instead of studying History.

But what is a Jew? Universal signifier
of wandering and displacement?
Stereotype of opulence, comfort,
while, simultaneously, the name
behind history's agitated isms?
If a Jew is a symbol of exile—
a symbol for others—
what is a Jew herself?

In the Symposium Room,
a visiting Jewish Studies professor explains everything
except the mystery
of his subject's survival.

# Poem on Our Eighteenth Anniversary

When you yelled, *Call them out*,
delirious in a head scarf and hospital gown,
the contraction monitor floating behind you.
When you rowed away from the shore at Bear Mountain,
our three daughters and two sons in the boat,
and I stayed behind on a bench
to grade essays.
When you withdrew your hand,
pretending not to see mine reach across the patch of grass
on the hill behind the dorms
where we sat, on a Sabbath afternoon,
two weeks into our first semester. When we lounged
on the student union's plastic-upholstered couch
after our first cafeteria shift
and discussed our classes.
When, a year later, in my college apartment,
study lamp illuminating your lovely face,
your hands slowly climbed my forearms.
When I hugged you at the top of the stairwell
before you took leave that first night—
familiar and strange
in your ponytail and cream cardigan—
and we drifted to sleep
in our respective apartments, twin buildings
standing side by side
in the upstate autumn air. When I returned home,
late at night, four years into our marriage,
on an adjunct's salary, no health insurance,
to find you sitting on the floor,
cleaning the drawer of the open fridge
in preparation for Passover,

your recently divorced brother asleep
on the apartment couch—
and you lifted your face,
excited to see me.
When, the year before we met,
at a college on another continent,
young men waited under the shade
of the lecture hall awning
to walk you to lunch.
When you took a bus, a subway, and then a second bus
to greet me at the gate, wearing red tights,
the first time I visited you between semesters.
When we kissed in Frick Park in the rain,
the restricted area of Albany International Airport,
in your pink childhood bedroom
when I had the flu,
in your college apartment after
the schnitzel and Moscato.
When you reached your hand out of our rowboat,
nineteen years later, to pluck a waterlily from Shepherds Lake.
When you sent me the Five Books of Moses,
the week before our wedding,
a note tucked inside the book of Genesis.
When I awoke from surgery,
and you sat at my bedside
in turquoise blouse and black skirt.
When you tossed a peanut butter cup through the air
and into my hands as you walked to the minivan
to drive the girls to drawing lessons,
your scarf—purple, aqua, maroon—lifted
by the January wind.
And today, when we sat on a bench
beside the Hackensack River, 18 years
into our marriage, sharing a bottle of lukewarm lime seltzer
you found in your purse,

and you told me about a ride you hitched
in the back of a flower truck
with two friends
your last summer in high school,
and I tried to picture that part of you
that would remain a stranger
leaning her lovely head
under swaying bouquets of yellow tulips.

## Driving Back to College in a Storm

And as I entered the onramp and the highway curved,
I realized I'd forgotten the Wayfarer's Prayer.

Rear tires backsplashed a wave
across my windshield. The universe blurred,

pinning me between a rock embankment
and a Greyhound bus.

When I came to, the nose of my Corolla
faced oncoming headlights, and the Greyhound was gone.

Because the evening was a surrealist,
a sponge cake my mother had packed in the trunk

stood upright on the highway pavement.
"A Hard Rain's A-Gonna Fall"

played from the speakers.
"It doesn't make any sense

that you are walking,"
the state trooper marveled,

resting a white glove
on the green sedan's mangled metal.

Three weeks later, I climbed a rented ladder
to your dormitory window, a poem

and ring in my breast pocket.
The wedding hall printed the afternoon groom's

scripted initials beside yours on our dinner mints—
a reminder that another nearly took my place.

## Poetry Readings

The one in the long narrow synagogue
beneath the elevated subway line. Oncoming trains
screeched over final stanzas. Poems
paused and resumed
as though first being written.

The one at an outdoor festival,
sandwiched
between bands:
Long-haired young men
thundered power chords,
then my thin voice echoed off pine trees
at the edge of the fairground,
the audience's confused faces.
The shirtless main attraction tuned up
in the middle of a sonnet
about shyness.

And the reading in the inner-city library's
poorly-lit basement.
Seven men and women
listening to a Chassidic Jew
recite lines about the Ein Sof
and life's great disappointments.

# IV

# There is Only One Story

*on the Pittsburgh synagogue shooting*

1.

There are always two stories:
That of the body, that of the soul,
plus the story of Cousin Reva,
who, arriving late that morning,
was instructed by an officer to wait things out
at the nearby public library.
*I feel guilty about not dying with my friends*,
she said the next day.

2.

It is October 27, 1988.
My friend Robert plays whiffle ball
in his backyard
abutting Tree of Life Synagogue.

It is October 27, 2018.
A stranger passes through
unlocked double doors.
Blocks away, Robert's son
begins his bar mitzvah portion:
Abraham inviting angels, wayfarers,
into his open tent.

*Perhaps*, Robert postulates,
*the soul of my recently deceased father interceded*
*on high, causing the news to be hidden*

*until his grandson had closed*
*the Torah scroll.*

And in the afternoon, the scroll is reopened,
and we read:
*And Abraham came to eulogize over Sarah*
*and to cry for her.*
And according to the hidden story—
the one the mystics tell—
Abraham represents the soul,
and Sarah the body.

3.

Now it is night. Half a block from the apartment where,
seventeen years earlier,
my wife and I lived when first wed, Jews of Pittsburgh
stand in the rain, holding candles. Eleven souls
ascend to the region of mystery
then swoop down to hover,
incandescently, over their former lives.

Away from the cameras and fanfare,
eleven bodies are ushered through
burial rituals—
pottery shards placed over twenty-two eyes,
eleven mouths.
Water poured to purify physical forms
that had, until recently, housed souls
whose last act on Earth was to whisper a prayer.

4.

There is only one story, say the mystics:
The souls of the Jewish people

throughout Jewish history
form one larger body.

The body bears more wounds
than we want to recall.
No one can explain how it limps forward
but has not faltered.

# The Visit

*Does it make me a bad Jew*
*in your eyes?*
he asked about attending services
only a few scattered Sabbaths,
cooking dairy and meat
in the same pots and pans.

I fingered the black knobs
on his sedan's passenger door,
stared at the sky's blue canopy
stretched over cornfields.

The previous morning,
we walked up a dirt road
then around a pond
where orange koi darted
out of widgeon grass
like flashes of clarity

and he spoke of his ex-wife's
suicide, his secret fears, his guilt.

The Baal Shem Tov taught,
a soul can descend
into a body, live
for seventy or eighty years,
for the purpose of performing
a particular favor
for another.

In his sunlit study,
I helped the poet wrap my tefillin
around his forearm
then secured the leather knot
over the long, graying hair
on the back of his head.

Now we rounded a curve
overlooking haystacks and silos
on the long drive
back to the airport.

Once, sensing an opening,
Moses asked to see the face
of the Divine—
to know the mystery of suffering,
the secret of sorrow.

Poised in the cleft of a rock,
Moses gazed up,
but the Divine Presence
had already passed by,
only the knot at the back of God's tefillin—
sign of the covenant—
still visible.

# Morning Prayer and the Waste Management Co.

*Did God withdraw*
*to make room for the universe*
*or merely carve out an open space*
*in His infinite light?*

asked the Chassidic discourse
I'd studied that morning,
standing at the open window,
wrapped in a prayer shawl and tefillin,
when the sanitation workers arrived
in their blue monogrammed overalls.

The men lifted the overstuffed cans
above their heads
and emptied the contents.
*Only the light was removed,*
the discourse answered.
*God's Essence is at home equally*
*in the sacred and the profane,*
*finite and infinite, and is, therefore,*
*always present.*

The sanitation workers
dropped the gray cans upside down
on the muddy grass.
*Then, in inverted fashion,*
*the world was created:*
*The way the wax indents*
*where the signet ring protrudes,*
*and protrudes where the ring indents.*
*The way the highest brick falls*
*farthest from the base of the wall.*

*That which appears ordinary, lowly,*
*is rooted more deeply in the Divine.*

I turned the next page
in my prayer book.
The sanitation workers
hung on to metal handles
and floated in the air.

# Women at Prayer

And I saw what must have been
a camp for young female Jewish artists
carrying canvases and paints,
wading, in long skirts,
into a field
past the community college library.
And when I looked up again
from my reading,
they were praying
in the high grass,
arms extended before their bodies,
prayer books held
toward the sky.

*

In the final hour of daylight, young women
at the Jewish night college in Brooklyn
recite the Afternoon Service—
rocking back and forth
in dim-lit stairwells, in alcoves,
in the aisles between library stacks,
in empty chemistry labs. A pause
between day job and evening class.
On their lips, prayers
for an ailing parent, an A
on an exam.

*

At dawn, decades ago,
I slipped out the yeshiva side door,
descended the steps
to the Wailing Wall,
and joined a quorum
of men at prayer.
From the room where prayer books
are stored when rain cascades
on the Western Wall Plaza,
we heard a voice pleading:

The widowed dentist in a navy headscarf
prayed for her sister
whose soul ascended
when she skied into a tree.

And the One who has seen the suffering
of their grandmothers
and great grandmothers
listened.
And what He was thinking
is history's great mystery.

# The Fragment of the Soul in the Body

*The soul has a story that has a shape that almost no*
*one sees. No, no one ever does.* —Marie Howe

1.

Light arcs like a highway
from the fraction of the soul in the body
back to the soul's source.

2.

No.
Not like a highway.

*Like a rope*, the mystics say.

The bottom strands, the soul in a body.
The top braids, the source of the soul fastened to Heaven's rafters. Tug
at either end
and the other moves.

Slightly.

3.

Or: The soul in the body is a ball chain tied

to the source of the soul—

the light bulb's toggle switch.

4.

The part of the soul that transcends the body
is an expert swimmer
backstroking through

the oceanic

heavens.

The soul in a body: captain of a nearly sinking ship,
the rudders outmoded,
the porthole fogged.

5.

But, the mystics say,
the transcendent part of the soul

was created for the fraction of the soul

enclothed in the body. The way an expert tutor is hired

for a struggling prince

on whose shoulders

the destiny of the kingdom depends.

# Chanukah: Kiel, Germany

*after a photograph by Rachel Posner*

On the sill of the Posner family apartment—
what else but a menorah?
And since this is late 1932, the window opens
to a view of—what else but?—a Nazi flag
hanging from the town hall's gray stones
on the opposite side of the street.
Akiva, his wife Rachel, their three children—
Gitta, Shulamit, Avraham Chaim—

absent from the photograph Rachel has snapped.
When darkness arrives, they will
step into the frame
to kindle the flames. The candles' symbolism almost too
obvious. The juxtaposition to the Swastika
almost cliché. But this isn't literature. Not
speculation. That a Jew walks down streets,
cooks dinner, reads the paper, sends letters

is remarkable given she is a member
of an eternal people. And here
is the eight-branched mitzvah object
on the eighth night—
the precise physical proportions, the blessings,
governed by finite rabbinic rules
to draw the infinite God into this shoe box
of a world. Like soul into body.
And note the couple's names:

The husband's that of the famous martyr
whose flesh Romans combed from his body.
The wife's that of the martyr's wife, who spent 24 years
of her marriage alone
so he could study the secrets
stored in the crowns of letters floating like ash
from the scrolls Roman officers set aflame.
This is 1932.
In four months, on the night following the boycott,

Akiva will risk his life
to provide Jewish burial for the body
of a young man who'd returned home for a visit,
shot as he crossed the threshold
of his parents' store. And the word for world—olam—
is rooted in the word helem,
which means the concealment of God.
And the number eight is one higher
than nature, one beyond the world
created in seven days. But we still have not found out
what six million means.

# Exile for the Sake of Redemption

The way a teacher, standing at the blackboard,
chalk in hand,
suddenly withdraws into himself
to follow the comet tail
of a thought
more profound than he has ever known—
then, after a long pause,
opens his eyes and returns
to his classroom
to share his discovery
with his students

is the way, the mystics say,
God, seemingly, recedes
back into Himself
until, suddenly,
after centuries,
redemption comes,
and a Divine light—
more radiant than the world
has ever known—
illuminates the universe
that thought it had been forsaken.

# V

## Notes on Marriage

The first week of the pandemic,
I delivered two bags of flour—
one whole wheat, one white—
to our elderly neighbors.
It was dusk, their home brightly lit.
Through the window,
I glimpsed the gray-haired man lifting his wife
into a dance.

*

*When wife and husband embrace and kiss,*
*their four arms spell*
*the feminine Divine name,*
*composed of four letters,*
*their four lips spell*
*the masculine Divine name,*
*composed of four letters.*

*

In the Galician village of Sokolova,
my wife's great grandfather
was known as the Roite Shochet,
the red-headed butcher.
His given name, Baruch,
his wife's, Bracha—
male and female
for blessing and blessing.

*

My wife placed a cup
of steaming coffee beside
a plate of buttered toast and scrambled eggs.
A blessing.
In my lunch box, the sandwich—
hummus, lettuce, cheese—
she prepared for my dinner.

*

I can't go back in time
to warn a dreamy-eyed teenager
not to fall for the saxophonist's
after-party promise. I can't
chance upon myself on the stairwell
at Taylor Allderdice High School
and explain patience.
Because God split the first couple
into male and female selves,
all our lives we ache
for wholeness.

*

An accordion wall
divided my wife's childhood bedroom
from the rest of her apartment.
A year of college overseas,
her first taste of freedom.
Mornings, young men waited at her door
with danishes and chocolate milk
in their outstretched hands.

*

Before creation, God divided
the feminine Divine light
from the masculine Divine light,
Shechina from Kudsha Brich Hu.
In the Messianic Era,
the two will reunite.

*

A compliment from a colleague,
a shared glance two subway stops from home.
Because the first couple
ate the fruit of confusion,
we desire those
who are not our other half.

*

May Hashem guard your goings and comings,
arrivals and departures,
your Netflix account,
your dining room table,
and your marital bed.

*

*After the prelude,*
*the embrace and the kiss,*
*the comingling*
*of the masculine and feminine names,*
*husband and wife reunite*
*as one flesh—*

*skin to skin*
*beneath a covering,*
*revealed and concealed,*
*as the Divine moves*
*beneath the veneer*
*of the physical world.*

*

Masking tape around the handles of our kitchen faucet,
a sister-in-law's hand-me-down dresses.
Why do you ask for so little?

Why did I marry a woman with a childlike streak?
And how, possessing that streak,
did you make it through the day we learned
our daughter had lost her hearing,
the years I barely looked up
from student papers?

*

Once, I saw a man in a navy suit and dark fedora
kneeling in the mud
at the edge of his wife's open grave.
He pled for forgiveness
while strangers
born across the ocean
lowered her body into the earth.

*

*If Sarah represents the body*
*and Abraham the soul,*
*why did God tell Abraham*
*to listen to Sarah's voice?*
*Because*, the mystics answer,
*in the Messianic Era,*
*we will see that the source of the body*
*is loftier than the source of the soul,*
*and so a soul descends into a body.*

*

One August night,
both 20,
we sat on your childhood bed,
backs against your pink bedroom wall,
the accordion divider half open,
and spoke of going
our separate ways.

*We will have a good life together*,
you said, raising your voice
over the AC's steady rumble.
*You will see.*

# NOTES

"Teachers and Students"

Section 4 includes a teaching drawn from Chapter Two of *Pirkei Avos*. Section 10 references the recorded classes of Rabbi Yehoshua B. Gordon, AH.

"Hearing Roy Orbison in a Mikvah in Salem, MA"

The second stanza alludes to a teaching mentioned in the Lubavitcher Rebbe's *Likkutei Sichos*, Volume 1, page 5.

"Notes on the Tzimtzum"

This poem was inspired by, and draws upon, the Rebbe Rashab's Chassidic discourse "V'Yadata Moscow, 5657."

"And I knew Everything Would Remain Ordinary"

The first stanza draws upon the Baal Shem Tov's conception of Divine Providence as elaborated on in Chabad teachings.

"There Is Only One Story"

Section 2 draws upon the Lubavitcher Rebbe's *Likkutei Sichos*, Volume 1, page 31.

"The Visit"

The final two stanzas refer to an episode in Exodus (32:33), where Moses requests to see God's face, but God replies that He will show Moses only His back. Borrowing from the Talmud (Brachos 7a), the commentator Rashi explains that, in this moment, God showed Moses the knot on His teffilin strap—a knot worshipers wear on the back of the head during morning prayers. Since, according to Jewish tradition, God does not possess a physical body or wear physical teffilin, this Talmud-based interpretation is understood on a spiritual level.

"Morning Prayer and the Waste Management Co."

This poem alludes to Rabbi Isaac Luria's teachings concerning the Tzimtzum. Whether to understand the Tzimtzum on a literal or non-literal level was the subject of a complex debate between early Chassidic leaders and their detractors. Chassidic thought posits that only the Or Ein Sof was concealed and not God's Essence.

The idea that the process of creation can be likened to the impression a signet ring leaves in wax is borrowed from the Alter Rebbe's *Tanya* ("Iggeret Hakodesh, Letter 20").

"Exile for the Sake of Redemption"

This poem was inspired by, and draws upon, a Chassidic teaching discussed in the Lubavitcher Rebbe's *Likkutei Sichos*, Volume 2, pages 360–363.

"Notes on Marriage"

Many of the italicized lines in this poem are drawn from *Reishes Chochma*, a 16th-century mystical work by Rabbi Eliyahu de Vidas. The penultimate stanza draws upon a teaching discussed in the Lubavitcher Rebbe's *Likkutei Sichos*, Volume 1, pages 33–34.

# ACKNOWLEDGMENTS

Thank you to the publications in which versions of the following poems first appeared:

*Anglican Theological Review*: "*I FELT LIKE I HAD WALKED THROUGH THE STREETS OF JERUSALEM IN AN EARLIER LIFE*"

*Baltimore Review*: "Teachers and Students"

*Breaking the Glass: The Laurel Review Contemporary Jewish Poetry Anthology*: "And I Knew Everything Would Remain Ordinary"

Chabad.org: "Exile for the Sake of Redemption"

*Cider Press Review*: "Morning Prayer and the Waste Management Co."

*Commonweal*: "This Summer Day"

*Harvard Divinity Bulletin*: "Women at Prayer"

*Ilanot Review*: "Re-creation Ex Nihilo Via Divine Utterance"

*Kosmos*: "In the Dream, My Father Reprimanded Me for Wearing Earmuffs Indoors"

*The Lehrhaus*: "The Deed," "Notes on the Tzimtzum," and "On the World's Continuity Via Divine Speech"

*Mizmor Anthology*: "Poetry Readings"

*New Voices: Contemporary Writers Confront the Holocaust*: "Chanukah: Kiel, Germany"

*The Paper Brigade*: "Universal Symbol"

*Paterson Literary Review*: "Impossibly," "Rabbi W.," and "Zaida Sydney"

*Pensive: A Global Journal of Spirituality and the Arts*: "Faith"

*Poetry International* (online): "There Is Only One Story"

*The Sun*: "The Buttonhook"

*Tiferet*: "Forty Years," "Notes on the Soul," "Ein Sof Radio," and "The Part of the Soul in the Body"

*Thrush*: "Prayer" and "Poem on Our Eighteenth Anniversary"

*TriQuarterly*: "What About the Here and Now?"

*Upstreet*: "The Visit"

*Vox Populi*: "Hearing Roy Orbison in a Mikvah in Salem, MA," "Notes on Marriage," and "Driving Back to College in a Storm."

"Exile for the Sake of Redemption" was reprinted in *Gashmius Magazine: Toward a Progressive neo-Hasidism.*

"Morning Prayer and the Waste Management Co." was reprinted in *Lubavitch International Magazine.*

"There Is Only One Story" was reprinted on Chabad.org.

"Re-creation Ex Nihilo Via Divine Utterance" was reprinted in *Best Spiritual Literature* (Vol. 8).

—

I would like thank Baruch November, Miriam Grossman, Rivkah Slonim, Phil Terman, and Liz Rosenberg for their encouragement and insightful suggestions that significantly improved this collection.

Thanks so much to David Caplan, cherished friend and mentor, for reading numerous drafts of the manuscript, providing sage advice, and guiding me through the twists and turns of yet another book.

Deepest gratitude to Gary Ickowicz for his fatherly advice, rich friendship, and abundant generosity.

Thank you to all my colleagues for supporting my work, and to my students for reminding me that poetry is a timeless gift that persists from one generation to the next. Thank you to Yetzirah: A Hearth for Jewish Poetry for providing the warmest of poetry families.

Thank you to the Slonims for their treasured guidance and inspiration. Thanks to my Morning Chassidus and Sunday Night Sicha groups.

Thanks to Luke Hankins of Orison Books for continuing to believe in my work and for ushering this book into print with editorial expertise and meticulous care. I am fortunate and grateful to be a member of the Orison family.

Thank you to my family—the Novembers and Reiches—for your support, warmth, and endless light. Thank you to my children, who inspire and teach me so much. May you be blessed with open and revealed goodness in all areas—always. And thanks most of all to Ahuva—muse, expert listener, model of patience, binding that holds the pages of the family book together.

This book is for my parents, Shimon and Chana November, and for David Caplan and Gary Ickowicz.

# ABOUT THE AUTHOR

Yehoshua November is the author of two previous poetry collections, *God's Optimism*, a finalist for The *Los Angeles Times* Book Prize, and *Two Worlds Exist*, a finalist for The National Jewish Book Award and The Paterson Poetry Prize. His poems have appeared in *The New York Times Magazine*, *The Sun*, *Prairie Schooner*, *Harvard Divinity Bulletin*, and *Virginia Quarterly Review*, as well as on the On Being podcast "Poetry Unbound." November teaches writing at Rutgers University and Touro University.

# ABOUT ORISON BOOKS

Orison Books is a 501(c)3 non-profit literary press focused on the life of the spirit from a broad and inclusive range of perspectives. We publish books of exceptional poetry, fiction, and non-fiction from perspectives spanning the spectrum of spiritual and religious thought, ethnicity, gender identity, and sexual orientation.

As a non-profit literary press, Orison Books depends on the support of donors. To find out more about our mission and our books, or to make a donation, please visit www.orisonbooks.com.

Orison Books is deeply grateful to our recurring annual donors for sustaining our important work. If you'd like to make a recurring or one-time contribution, please visit www.orisonbooks.com/support-us.

**Sustainers' Circle**

Carol Dines
Michele Laub
Laura & Barry Rand
Bruce Spang
Lee Stockdale
Anonymous

**Advocates' Circle**

David Ebenbach
Anonymous

**Supporters' Circle**

Nickole Brown
Richard Chess

**Friends' Circle**

Paige Gilchrist
Laurel Haavik
Alida Woods